TRT
Ministries
Crowned With Royalty,
That We Might Live In
The Kingdom.

Isaiah 62:6

A Project of TRT Ministries

P.M.S. (POWER, MONEY & SEX)

P.M.S. (POWER, MONEY & SEX)

Scripture quotations marked KJV are taken from the King James Version of the Bible.

P.M.S. Power, Money & Sex 2nd Edition
ISBN-13: 978-0-9971704-2-9
Copyright© 2018 by Tommy R. Twitty
Tommy R. Twitty Ministries
P.O. Box 613
Chesnee, SC 29323

Library of Congress Control Number: 2018905994

P.M.S. (POWER, MONEY & SEX)

Table of Contents

P.M.S. Continued

P.M.S. (POWER, MONEY & SEX)

Introduction

In Genesis chapter 3:1 – 11 in the EXB translation it depicts the event which interrupted the rest of God and what caused one man to lose the covenant relationship that God had created. In verse one it begins with the defining of the serpent and it says that it was clever, shrewd, cunning and crafty. The snake is like the individual that sees you going through something and comes to you saying, if you were with me, you wouldn't have to worry about the things on your mind because I would treat you better and I would do more for you. Any person that approaches an individual with that line male or female is a snake. How can they offer you more when they don't know where you are or who you are? The serpent approached Eve and once she allowed it to entertain her with a question, (Gen: 1b "Did God really say that you must not eat fruit from any tree in the garden") and she responded to it, she had already begun to entertain something God had previously warned her not to do. Why did the woman answer the snake and where was man. The Bible says that every man is tempted when he is lured, drawn out or pulled away by his own lust and the day that this happens they will call lust, love. They will have a desire for it in the name of love. Eve had a desire to know and in Genesis 3:2 EXB, Eve had even added to what God had instructed man and woman concerning the tree.

V. 2 - *The woman answered the snake [3:1], "We may eat fruit from the trees in the garden. ³ But God told us, 'You must not eat fruit from the tree that is in the middle of the garden [the tree of the knowledge of good and evil]. You must not even touch it [Eve was adding to the divine command], or you will die.'*

Because Eve's eyes were being opened through deception, Eve would now have worldly intelligence and she would take on the mind of the snake. Eve would become cunning and because of this deceit, the woman's eyes came open and she saw that the tree was beautiful, pleasing to the eyes, that its fruit was good to eat for food, and that it would make her wise. So Eve took of the fruit and gave it to her husband who was with her. Man had apparently been silent while the wife was speaking to a snake, "and he ate it." Gen. 3:6 EXB

It's as if literally their eyes came open and they both realized that they were naked, so being wise, and knowing that there is provision where God is, they sewed fig leaves together and made something to cover themselves. Upon hearing the sound of God walking in the garden during the cool part of the day, man and woman had hid themselves. So what does this mean for us? The majority of us know the story. From that story and those events came consequences. Consequences that we must acknowledge still exist today. The purpose in discussing this passage is to gather clarity on those events and to accept the consequences of your yesterday so that you can better prepare for tomorrow.

When you are entering into a relationship it may seem easy to accept some things because you are a "Christian" although those things may not fit your character and expectations, but that is not what you do. You need to be honest about who you are and learn to say it's not okay and if you are not what they want, you accept them leaving. It's necessary in all things that you get an understanding, "always know the end before the beginning," because it will tell you where the relationship is going. Adam assumed nothing because God presented him with the woman and he chose to eat of the fruit. It is preeminent in all relationships; dating, marriage, business, religious and so on that you seek and obtain wisdom. The Bible tells us that the beginning of wisdom is to fear the Lord. Having good understanding wins favor from others.

Chapter 1

God's Original Blueprint for Man & Woman

God's original blueprint for man and woman in the state of singleness was to first reveal unto the man and woman their identities. The first thing that God did for man was to form him out of the dust of the ground, and He then shaped him into his own image; Gen 1:26-27

(Chapter Ref. Gen 2:7-8; 15-18; 20-24 AMP)

The second thing God did was to take the man that He had formed in his image and make him into his likeness. The third thing he did was to breathe into man's nostrils, making man a living soul. The word form represented man's negative image but after He formed man's image, He then created man into His likeness which is the proof or the positive of man. This process is similar to taking a picture. The camera opens its lens and uses its shutter to take the picture. The flash goes off to illuminate and capture the negative image of an individual and brings it back. As the shutter closes the lens allows the captured image to be placed on the film. The photographer then takes the negative film into the dark room and develops it into the positive (the proof) or into the likeness of what we see.

The Bible says that God planted a garden called Eden for the man. A place full of delight, pleasure and fulfillment: "the spot". He gave man a new responsibility and with this new responsibility, God gave man dominion, power and authority over the earth so that man would subdue it, be fruitful, multiply and increase.

Then God gave man a ministry and an assignment. At this point God took everything that He had ever created and placed man over it, to manage it and to be steward over it. Next, we find that God began to have a conference call in the heavens or He literally spoke to those in the heavens to say that it is not good for man to be alone. Man was single, but not lonely. He then brought all of the animals to man to see what man would name them but for Adam there was no companion (Gen. 2:18a).

God put Adam to sleep and took woman from man's side or rib. He presented the woman to the man and Adam describes her as "bone of my bone and flesh of my flesh" (Gen. 2:21-23).

The word single means to be whole, mature, and complete. It also means oneness. This is why the Bible says that when Adam and Eve came together they became one not two (Gen. 2: 24). This simply means that they became Godly soul-mates. The union of a man and a woman does not make them whole. If the male or female does not come into the relationship whole as an individual then being in a relationship will not make them whole or make them one.

Man and woman become one because they have equality in sharing the same vision, the same responsibility, the same assignment and the same destiny because the responsibility God gave Adam in the beginning is now the same responsibility placed on Eve. It's only when the relationship no longer experiences equality that a God-ordained relationship becomes divided. In Mark 3:25 the Bible says, "A house that is divided against itself, that house cannot stand." When Eve lost focus in regard to her responsibility and assignment she caused a division within the house. The reason she lost focus and became distracted was that she began to seek out more power and influence from Satan the serpent who deceived her. Romans 12:3 says, "For I say, through the grace given to me, to every man that is among you, not to think of himself more highly than he ought to think..." It was when Eve thought of herself more highly then she ought to; by seeking out more power, which she did when she ate from the forbidden tree. It was her need for power that brought destruction to her relationship and caused her to lose focus in fulfilling her assignment.

God, unlike man, started with nothing but He saw the potential. A relationship is a process and in the beginning it may look like nothing but God knows the potential of man choosing his helpmeet. In this process called a relationship you will continue to see the negative image of man until you remember the uniqueness or the likeness of God that you know is within that person. When you're connected to the right person, the two of you become what wasn't because you always had the potential to become what you are supposed to be. However, you needed the one who understood your uniqueness and likeness to help you discover who you are as individuals and as a couple.

The first gift God gave to man was Himself; you will never understand yourself until you've been with someone that understands you better than you do. The person that you are meant to be with understands your uniqueness even when there is nothing going on.

The second gift God gave man was His presence in the Garden of Eden; Eden was a gift to man. Earlier, we identified something that was called "the spot" and to bring further clarity we want you to consider Eden as "the spot". As long as you stay in that spot no weapon formed against you will prosper. In that spot you will experience moments. Moments are times when we experience God's favor and blessings. As long as we stay in the spot we will continue to be in the presence of God.

P.M.S. (POWER, MONEY & SEX)

Let's take a minute to explain the meaning of God's "work" for man. God commanded man to do work and before Adam would ever know Eve he understood that man was to work."Work" is different from a job where you go and receive training for a particular skill and then perform this skill at someone else's place of business. Work from God is our ministry or business. It is our ability to produce or to provide for those God has entrusted in our care. God intended for man to work for himself, to work the gift which God gave him with authority, dominion, and power. The "work" that God gave us is what we were born to do and even when you die the work goes on. The double portion is that your heirs will reap the benefits of your work.

God planted Adam in the Garden of Eden which He had made for him. In the Garden He planted provisions with one stipulation. In Genesis 2:16-17 NKJV, He tells Adam that he may freely eat of every tree in the garden except for the tree of the knowledge of good and evil. He was not to eat of this tree and if he did he would surely die.

In the Garden the ground worked for Adam to produce what he wanted and what he saw a need for. When you "work," the ground will always work for you and when you have a job you will always work for the ground and with this understanding, man is successful in the Garden and in his relationship with God. Man recognizes that he is in "the spot"; he knows God's presence, the gifts given to him by God, he understands the culture of God, he understands the environment, and he understands how to be blessed, how to be fruitful. It's only when a man does not understand these things that he should be alone.

What godly woman wants a man who does not know his purpose? A real man only needs a helpmeet when he knows who he is. God brought animals to man so that man could choose his helpmeet. Adam named every animal but they were not suitable for man so Adam waited for his helpmeet and while he waited he kept doing ministry.

In Genesis 2:21-22KJV, God does surgery on the man and out of man he birthed woman. She was not formed like man was formed but she was birthed out of man or made from man. Woman comes from the weaker side of man, the side where his heart is. When God made her, He made her with curves, because He knew that man was the foundation but woman was the structure of man and was made for his foundation.

P.M.S. (POWER, MONEY & SEX)

We all know that man is the head and this comes from the fact that man is the foundation but every great builder understands that no structure can stand unless it has a good foundation, a firm foundation. So what does this mean for relationships? The enemy, Satan, is after the foundation. He wants man because a structure can't stand without a foundation.

When you remove a man from a relationship with a woman, God's structure for man begins to fall. Woman was created to cover man's heart. She is affectionate and detailed but she is not the foundation. She must understand that a man is not interested in feelings all the time so to build a relationship she must know how to cover her foundation. No man wants to hear all the details from a woman without having his needs met first. In a relationship a man must fulfill the **"Five P Factors."**

1st is Priest: Man must cover his house and minister to his family.

2nd is Prophet: Man must point the way or the direction in which his household is going.

3rd is Protector: Man must protect his home.

4th is Provider: It is man's responsibility to bring provisions to his home.

5th is Pleaser: It is man's responsibility to please those in his home but it was not until Eve pleased Adam that he was able to fulfill all of his responsibilities. For this reason, God created male and female.

The word man is considered spiritual while male is considered flesh, just as woman is considered spiritual and female flesh. A male has sexual factors or desires and females are more affectionate but until a woman learns how to fulfill the sexual desires of her man, she will continue to have affections and a man that will not be able to listen.

Relationships are a strategic part of the kingdom and it was never intended for man to be with a number of females; it was always purposed for him to find his wife. Although they are two individuals and single, the two shall become one. When two come into an agreement or relationship, a covenant is always established and to establish a covenant, blood must be shed and this is why women bleed when they have sex for the first time. This is why they were to marry before having sex. Having sex was to be a sign of their confession and agreement to establish a covenant.

P.M.S. (POWER, MONEY & SEX)

Proverbs 18:22 NKJV, says that "when a man finds a wife, he finds a good thing and obtains favor." His wife is presented to him by God as being the one chosen by the Father. When God presents the woman, they are back in "the spot". If you can imagine, Adam is awake and he sees two people coming toward him. He recognizes the woman and says this is bone of my bone, flesh of my flesh. It is this relationship that God originally planned. It is this relationship that He favors. In Proverbs, the word "finds" means that when a man discerns his wife, when he sees her, he will know her and understand her. He will understand her hurt and her pain. This is why he can call her his bone. It's important to note that when a man finds his wife he immediately obtains favor, everything becomes fruitful and multiplies and he realizes his vision and purpose.

So what caused this oneness to be broken? Adam and Eve shared their honeymoon suite (Eden) with a snake. They let someone come in who should have never been allowed to speak over, speak in or speak to their relationship. Man and woman became vulnerable and they strayed from the presence of God. They left "the spot". You can lose everything when you leave the presence of God and any man out of the presence of

P.M.S. (POWER, MONEY & SEX)

God will find it hard to fulfill a woman because he will not know his purpose.

Chapter 2

Where You At?
(Stop Playing the Blame Game)

When man and woman got out of the presence of God, it interrupted and disturbed the rest of God. It caused God to issue out a cease and desist order, that is to say, stop everything that you are doing until you are legally authorized to start back up again. When man and woman intentionally tried to hide from the presence of God it caused all of earth and creation to go into a catastrophic disturbance.

"And they heard the sound of the Lord God walking in the garden in the cool of the day, so the man and his wife hid and kept themselves hidden from the presence of the Lord God among the trees of the garden."

Adam and Eve represented the first family. They were the first public unhealthy relationship to have a dispute and a disagreement with God and even after the sin they had committed; God the Father, came to offer man and woman fatherly marital counseling, but instead of accepting responsibilities as man and woman in a relationship, they blamed one another for what went wrong instead of owning up to their own mistakes.

Why is it that man and woman instead of allowing God the Father to give them marital counseling, hid from His presence? They took a healthy relationship and caused it to become unhealthy. This in turn interrupted their uninterrupted ministry and their uninterrupted life. When God had to go out and seek for man and woman, they hid from the Creator. The one who had created them and put them in creation, but yet and still he asked man "where are you?" God wanted to hear from man and when Adam responds that they hid themselves because they were afraid and naked, God has more questions. "Who told you that you were naked and what have you done?" Have you done what I warned you not to do?

In posing the first question of where are you, God is asking every man and woman why they have left the place and presence of God. Why have you abandoned and neglected your responsibilities? Why have you neglected your gift and your position in life? What would make you cancel the anointing on your life and disqualify yourself from the assignment that I had for your life? Man and woman were already in relationship with God and because they chose to leave the place that God created for them, they cancelled the plans that God had for their relationship.

Man and woman chose to leave the place called Eden, a place of pleasure and delight. A place that represents the spot and environment that God created for man and woman to cultivate a kingdom environment and because they did this, God had to do what any parent would do when they can't find their children. God put out an A. P. B., an all points bulletin to search for the lost man and woman who had hidden themselves from His presence, and He asked man "where are you?"

P.M.S. (POWER, MONEY & SEX)

In any relationship it's more important to get an understanding than it is to make sure that someone knows that you love them. So God asked man and woman another question in order to metaphorically get an understanding. So God asked man and woman the second question, who told you that you were naked? He says to them who have you been talking and listening too? Who is it that has given you wrong counseling and wrong direction? Who is it that has caused you to disconnect from Me, from our relationship? Knowing in totality what had been done, God asked a rhetorical question of man and woman. He asked, "What have you done?" God, being our Father, and like any concerned parent in a relationship with their child, asked man and woman have you done what I warned you not to do? God asked man and woman did they understand the totality of what they had done, when they did what He warned them not to do. Man and woman had taken themselves out of the presence of God and now they were about to evicted from the Garden of Eden, the place their Father had created for them.

P.M.S. (POWER, MONEY & SEX)

Why did God ask these questions of man and woman? Did God want to know more about them or did He want to see, how they would respond to His inquiry? Neither of these answers why God asked the questions, but it leads us to learn more about how God could create man and woman, knowing what they would do, when He had already warned them not to do it.

Man was created by God in three parts: body, spirit and soul. Before God favored man to find his wife, man first as a single had to prove to God he could be successful and faithful in his responsibilities to have an uninterrupted ministry until he was ready for a wife and family. Man had to demonstrate to the Father that he could be trusted and that he understood what he was assigned to do in the relationship and in the body that God had created.

To understand what God intended for our relationships we must know the 3 Levels of understanding needed for each level of connection to have successful relationships.

P.M.S. (POWER, MONEY & SEX)

1st level of an "Understanding Connection Agreement" is called a Spiritual level of connection. The Spirit is part of the "P" or Power in understanding relationships.

2nd level of an "Understanding Connection Agreement" is the Physical and Social Connection. The Body which represents the "M" or Money of P.M.S. This will be better explained later, but to help you understand; money is tied to the physical and social connections, decisions and arrangements that we have in life.

3rd level of an "Understanding Connection Agreement" is the Mental and Emotional Connections, which are tied to the "S" or sex of the acronym P.M.S. and that is our Soul.

It is important to introduce each of these three levels of understanding to the 2nd edition of this book. P.M.S. or power, money and sex are the driving forces of any relationship. Many have entered into relationships for what they believed is love and not with an understanding. Any business partnership or relationship is established with an understanding. You don't just give someone a million dollars and expect that they will invest it for you without understanding what it is that you are entering into, although some exclusions apply. However, for the purpose of this book and its discussion on relationships, let us begin with Amos 3:3 EXB. "Two people will not walk together unless they have agreed to do so." Therefore two people that would walk together in disagreement would create a mismatch or what the Bible says in 2 Corinthians 6:14 EXB, they would be unequally yoked. 2 Corinthians says, "Do not join yourselves to [become partners with; be mismatched/unevenly yoked with] unbelievers." Suffice to say, do not join together with someone that you are not in agreement with or someone that you don't have an understanding with. It does not recommend that you enter into fellowship, partnership or relationship with someone that you cannot first come to an agreement with. Light and darkness cannot come together because light will always cause the dark to fade away because light and darkness are never in agreement.

P.M.S. (POWER, MONEY & SEX)

How can we walk together except we agree? Why would you enter into a lifelong contract without a "Relationship Understanding Connection Agreement" (RUCA)? The RUCA is an agreement that tests the levels of understanding in a relationship and like any other test what you don't pass, you fail. So would you hire someone that fails the test you give them to see if they are qualified to do a job? Would you be in a partnership with someone who did not agree that they were going to do half the work? If not, then why would you be in relationship with someone that you did not have an understanding connection agreement with concerning your relationship, engagement or marriage?

So let's test the levels of understanding in your relationship or in the relationship that you are about to enter into. The 1st test level reveals if the person that you desire to have a future relationship with can pass the Spiritual level of connection. This first level tests whether or not you share the same vision or the same belief. It tests whether or not your goals and purpose are the same and if you share the same GOD.

P.M.S. (POWER, MONEY & SEX)

It will reveal whether or not you are willing to share the same covenant agreement, the same values and create the same blueprint for your lives and the lives of your children, should you have any. When considering if there is a spiritual level of connection you'll want to know how you're going to build a balanced relationship so that the two of you can do successful ministry and life together without playing tug-a-war and pulling one another in different directions.

The 2nd level of an Understanding Connection Agreement is the Physical and Social connections, and these connections deal with the body. In order to have clarity in the decision making process and in choosing whether or not to spend the rest of your life with this one person; you need to know from both a physical and a social understanding where they are. You need to know, what is their level of health, how are they doing medically and what's their medical history? Do you have income and financial awareness of this individual's finances? Do you know their financial history? How much debt they are in and when do they intend on paying this debt off? If they intend on paying this debt off how and when will they pay this debt off? What is their financial plan? Will they have money in the future or will they constantly be paying off old debt? Before you sign-off on a promissory proposal agreement to be connected with this person in the future you should know where they stand and if they have any long term diseases or ailments. If someone is proposing to you, they are asking for you to sign a promissory agreement to do life together. If you are proposing to be with someone you have a right to have a plan in place before the promissory agreement is signed. To have a physical and social level of connection you must be willing to reveal to one another the expectations of your (Do's and Don'ts), (likes and dislikes), the things that you are willing to do and the things that you are not willing to do. It's important to share and know these things to avoid misunderstandings, when you are planning on building a future together without any interruptions.

The person that you are going to be with from a P.M.S. perspective must also be aware of your sexual preferences and expectations along with knowing your sex drive and desires from each other. If you looked at your female partner and desired her because of the body that she had, then you should clarify that's what you like and in five years you still want that body. If you started the relationship off and you were use to having sex four times a week, then by all means the agreement can't just change up because later one partner doesn't feel like it. You signed a promissory agreement.

Proverbs 5:19 – 21 in the VOICE translation says "she who is lovely as a deer and graceful as a doe-as you drink in her love, may her breasts satisfy you at all times. My son, why get caught up in some other woman and embrace the breasts of a stranger? Wisdom recognizes the beauty of sexual intimacy. After all, God designed us as sexual beings. But for physical intimacy to retain the beauty of its design, it must be shared wisely. It is meant to be shared with someone who is your own." In marriage two become one, so they belong together and belong to each other. In that safe place of belonging, one finds fulfillment. So a husband or a wife must partake only of the partner's body and love. To seek intimacy elsewhere is foolish. "You see, the Eternal sees our ways before Him. He watches every move we make and knows where those paths lead." Before you say you do, you need to be able to say I will.

The problem with any relationship is that we go in believing that we can change someone and when it does not turn out the way we expect we continue to call on God. Why? Because we will always call on God to get us out of something that we did not understand and therefore did not plan for. We can only do what we agreed upon and anything else doesn't work.

The 3rd level of understanding deals with the greatest challenge and struggle for relationships. It's the lack of understanding at this level that hurts relationships in church, in business and in the natural. We cannot spiritualize where our feelings and emotions have gotten us into trouble and caused us to be broken. Some of the strongest spiritual people in the word are the weakest because they are fragile mentally and emotionally.

P.M.S. (POWER, MONEY & SEX)

This third level of understanding deals with the mental and emotional connection, the Godly vs. ungodly soul connection. The thing you must know at this third level of understanding is that you must be willing to ask the right questions and to gather all of the information concerning the person you are planning on being in partnership with or in relationship with. If you are in a partnership or business relationship, at this level you would consider the stability of the mind of those you are coming in agreement with. Can they make sound decisions? Do they have the evidence to support their suggestions or to back up their findings? You must do a mental and emotional background check concerning their past, their present and your future with them. You cannot talk about a future with someone that you do not know their past and present, and perhaps someone that still wants to live in their past and present. If you choose to make this business deal, is it because this person is offering something for your future not to fulfill a fantasy or dream of their past endeavors? When doing this you don't need a feeling, a drive or an emotion, because it's those feelings and emotions that have gotten you in trouble before and because you have not dealt with these feelings before do not try to jump over them now. It's important to know all parties and partners when you are planning to share a future build a business or start a ministry. You do not act like the past and present did not occur or that mistakes did not happen but you do not make it the past and present your future.

The first connection test when it comes to dealing with mental and emotional soul connections is discovering the person that you are planning on sharing your future with. You should know the mental and emotional state of mind of everyone in the relationship. What is their maturity and immaturity level? If you are considering a personal relationship and desiring to share a future they must work out their own soul salvation according to the word of God. You cannot fix their past issues or their present mistakes. The soul connection exposes the character of a person when they are under pressure. As Maya Angelou so eloquently spoke, "when someone shows you who they are believe them; the first time," because the pressures of life will expose who that person really is.

P.M.S. (POWER, MONEY & SEX)

The character of a person is not demonstrated when things are always going right, but pressure reveals a person's true identity. It reveals how they are when things go wrong. Many times when dealing with soul connections of a person or the mental and emotional hurt and pain tolerance you may discover to late in the relationship, that the individual or person may have suppressed previous childhood and adulthood brokenness and wounds that sometimes resurface over time because they have lived the majority of their life in denial, but in reality they are still fractured and broken. They have lived most of their life with mental and verbal abuse from their childhood experiences that still impact their past and present relationships. They have birthed ungodly soul ties and connections that have been passed down from generations for some. This cycle or soul tie continues to show up because you thought you were over it, but you're still dealing with the mental and verbal abuse from adults that occurred from generation to generation. The problem is that we can't hide or mask our soul forever. A broke soul always entertains more sounds or things that we cannot see or hear because until a person deals with their past and present they cannot move forward.

At this third level of connection, the relationship is headed for trouble with massive problems that are happening sooner rather than later. These problems will continue to birth inconsistencies highlighting immaturity, dysfunction, brokenness, jealousy, insecurities, anger, temper tantrums, and other mental and verbal signs of inconsistency. These signs will prove they are immature mentally, broken emotionally and that they struggle with a broken mindset and an ungodly soul-tie connection. Make sure that you do not plan to share your future relationship, business or partnership with Dr. Jekyll and Mr. Hyde. Too many times people make the mistake in their relationship dealing with the Dr. Jekyll and Mr. Hide Syndrome, where a person is one way sometimes and then acts another way at other times. This is caused by a fragile state of mind and it is because they are still holding on to their past childhood brokenness from mental and verbal abuse. The brokenness of both past childhood and present adulthood has caused them to have a broken soul. It causes them to suppress multiple personalities, bi-polar conditions, and suppressed emotions and to seek out relationships that they can control or that they will verbally, physically and spiritually lead. In a relationship before you say "I Do," say "I will" get an understanding of all the levels of understanding.

Scripture References:
Genesis 3:1 – 11 EXB
Genesis 3:8 AMP
Genesis 3:11a VOICE
Genesis 3:11b TLB
Genesis 3:23 EXB
Genesis 2:7 AMP
Proverbs 18:22 NKJV
Genesis 2:21 – 23 VOICE
3 John 1:2 AMP
Amos 3:3 EXB
2 Corinthians 6:14 EXB
Proverbs 5:19 – 21 VOICE

Chapter 3

Buyer's Remorse

In many relationships we have "Buyer's Remorse", we get excited about obtaining or paying on something but we don't have a plan to pay it off. So in relationships we get excited about being in a relationship but we don't understand the cost and the upkeep of that relationship. This is where friendship, business and love gets tricky. We have become drunken by the love, but now that we are awakening from this love drunken state, we realize the relationship is in debt and we can't pay it off. This reality in a relationship is similar to that of purchasing a $30,000 vehicle because the sound system was good, but when you drove off the lot it was a lemon.

In Gen 29:15 – 25 EXB, Laban, Jacob's uncle says to him you are my family and I cannot let you work for free. Jacob asked for Rachel's hand in marriage. In the agreement, Jacob says I will work seven years for free. He told Laban that he would not have to do anything but allow him to marry Rachel in seven years.

P.M.S. (POWER, MONEY & SEX)

Jacob was so in love with Rachel that he was willing to invest the time for the beauty of Rachel and in this time it seemed like only a few days to Jacob. When the seven years was up, Jacob went to Laban and asked for Rachel to be his wife. Laban gave a celebration and tricked Jacob by giving him Leah. Jacob was so in love that he went in to consummate his relationship with Rachel, but did not realize that Laban had given him Leah. How can you be so in love with someone or so blinded by a relationship that you don't know who they are in the dark? The revelation of Leah being in the tent, caused Jacob to ask Laban what have you done, but Jacob was so in love with Rachel and so blinded he did not have an understanding of what was going on.

Relationships are predicated on understanding the terms and the terms are what you have sworn off on, by indicating "I Do, I will, or we agree." You can't get a loan from the bank and once you see the bill discover the terms are not what you agreed too. Don't get into a relationship so someone else can brag about your trophy and you can't pay for it. In all thy getting, get an understanding. The reason Jacob could not tell the difference between the body of the one that he was in love with and the one that he did not want was because he was drunk. He was intoxicated.

Once daylight came Jacob was suffering from buyer's remorse. When Laban indicated that he wanted Jacob to be with Rachel that was false advertisement. Laban wanted the free labor and would say anything to get it. To avoid buyer's remorse, you have to know and understand who and what you are getting.

Many of you have taken an early test drive of your relationship and it was good, but now you are suffering with buyer's remorse. You want to drive the relationship that you are in back up on the car lot and leave it there, but before you say "I Do" to someone or before you cut covenant or sign a promissory agreement make sure you are 100% sure. Make sure that you know their strengths and weaknesses, their emotional state, their social mindset, their business acumen and their spiritual relationship with God. When you buy a car you may be able to take it back, but when you cut covenant and enter into a marriage contract you cannot trade or exchange him or her in because they are a lemon.

Jacob had buyer's remorse after he had slept with Leah and he wanted to give her back to Laban, but he couldn't.

Chapter 4

Toxic & Dysfunctional Relationships

Do you love helping people? Have you ever been in love, but have been stressed out with the relationship? Have you ever wanted to strangle someone you loved? Do you feel that you need to pray and ask God for more love? Many people will answer these questions indicating that they do not need more love. In your mind you don't have a problem loving people. Your problem is understanding people. It's hard to help people that you love because it hurts so badly. The problem is that those, whom you are assigned to help, don't want your help and its making the love you have for people to turn on them. It's not that you have a love problem, its understanding that you are assigned to help. It's your inability to accept that you are only assigned to help their weaknesses. If God has called you to help people, it's not because of their strength. You are assigned to understand and help their weakness and then to move on. When you don't understand that you are not assigned to love them you are assigned to help them, you will stop being damaged by life.

P.M.S. (POWER, MONEY & SEX)

Jesus himself had to understand the terms of His relationship to the world. If you are not following God, He is not going to get back up on the cross and die again because you did not understand the agreement. We can't get mad at people because they do not receive us, nor can we put stipulations upon our love. We are to help them in the name of Christ or for the sake of the business, not in the name of love. It's our agreement with Jesus Christ that we must understand our relationship with Him. If we don't understand the agreement, then we will want those that we love to change out of our anger and "love", but not out of purpose.

Toxic and dysfunctional relationships begin and end because we entered into a relationship with an agenda that was not God's. Many times we involve ourselves in personal relationships because of emotions or feelings and we lack the mindset to get an understanding because our flesh feels good. In business we enter into relationships with business partners that can help us achieve one situation, but it does not help us in all of our future business endeavors. This lack of understanding accountable creates chaos in the work environment because the partners are no longer working in tandem, but they are dysfunctional. In ministry we seek to help people, but when we do not consider whether or not we are assigned to help the people that we want to help. When we fail to have an understanding in any relationship, we are setting the relationship up to become toxic and fail. A toxic relationship is one that is poisonous and can become deadly as we know by the sheer volume of domestic abuse cases in America. Toxic relationships are not limited to personal relationships, they can be found in business, community and ministry. A toxic relationship is one that does not have understanding of the roles that each person must play and when the roles become reversed it wreaks havoc on the relationship no matter what type.

Chapter 5

Baby Mama Drama, Baby Daddy Drama

In understanding the statistics for this chapter, we wanted to insure that there was no bias. This is important because the discoveries have led to statistics pointing out that there are more women suffering from life's struggles and problems than men. The statistics have led us to the conclusion that the governmental and economical system was designed for our men to fail and our women to have to trust in a system that would attempt to replace the man for as long as they wanted it too.

Are you aware that many people enter into relationships where one partner already has kids and the two adults decide to get married, but they never consider the kids? They take a vow to one another, but the kids don't get to take an oath or a vow. The majority of the time kids have no input in the adult's decision to get married they just have to accept the decision to have a step parent and step siblings. Marriage, business, or ministry should not be entered into lightly and all aspects and individuals should be considered before saying yes. If you are just getting married to play games with your ex then you are harming your children and you are unable to see it because you are so stuck on hurting your ex that you are willing to risk hurting your own children.

Someone that is a Baby Mama is a female who is mad at the fact that she can't have her ex back, so she takes on many negative attributes; such as being spiteful, jealous or even crazy. She takes on the responsibility of making the relationship with a child or children difficult at every chance she gets. A "Baby Mama" does not care if she hurts her own children in the process, but she is not a woman, she's a "baby mama." However, a woman that knows the relationship is over and has no hard feelings, works with you and compromises. She is consistent so that both of you have a lasting and healthy relationship with your child (ren). A real mother works to get along with her ex for the sake of their child or children.

In the United States today, there are nearly 13.6 million single parents raising over 21 million children. Single fathers are far less common than single mothers, constituting 16% of single-parent families. According to Single Parent Magazine, the number of single fathers has increased by 60% in the last ten years, and is one of the fastest growing family situations in the United States. 60% of single fathers are divorced. While fathers are not normally seen as primary caregivers, statistics show that 90% of single-fathers are employed, and 72% have a full-time job.

These statistics are in line with what we see in society. It shows how the system has lied and manipulated the family structure to get our women to depend more on the system, while the system has removed our men from the home to incarceration. This was a plan designed by the system to destroy what God has ordained and designed. It is the trick of the enemy to separate the family and to methodically break down what God created as a beautiful institution, the family.

Over 9.5 million American families are run by single mothers and it has been statistically proven that the lack of social support for our single mothers has caused them to spiral into depression. Studies show that our single mothers are more likely to have mental issues; financial hardships live in a low income area and receive low levels of social support. All of these factors have been taken into consideration when evaluating the mental health of our single mothers. The occurrence of moderate to severe mental disability was more pronounced among single mothers at 28.7% compared to partnered mothers at 15.7% (co-parenting done by two people, not necessarily a man and a woman). These mental disabilities have caused anxiety disorders and chronic depression for our single mothers. Women, ages 15 – 24, are more likely to live in a low socio-economic area and are statistically more likely to become pregnant while in high school, drop out or quit and never achieve their high school diploma or get their GED certificate. Studies and research have discovered there is a different outcome for a single mother versus a single woman without a child. There is a difference between married women that are mothers versus those that are separated and divorced and now struggle with the responsibilities of raising their child or children by themselves. It is more likely that this mother, the separated and divorced mother; will struggle with psychiatric disorders, but a single mother that has never been married with children deals and copes better with her condition than that of a woman that has been married and then separated or divorced. The mother that has been married and divorced has a higher likelihood to fall into different types of addictions and bad habits cause personality disorders and even PTSD (Post Traumatic Stress Disorder). A single mother that has become overwhelmed with the raising of her child or children alone can have mental health issues that may make her a victim or a high risk candidate for multiple levels of depressive systems. The mother that has been married may suffer because it is likely that she was part of a two income lifestyle and now she is suppose to continue making it work, when her lifestyle has been snatched away. She trusted in that two income household, but not in God.

The church expects women to just come to the church and get happy in the spirit when these women are dying and we are not doing anything to help them. We tell them to shout over it and it will work out, but we have to do better. We have a responsibility to have this difficult conversation. These single mothers and unmarried wives have turned to a man or a system that says it will take care of them. This same system infers that if you ever go back to a man and try to have a relationship we will cut you off. You can lose your housing, food stamps and any other benefits if you let a man in the home, but we, the church; tell them to get over it while the enemy is targeting the young women at the age of 15. We thank God for every woman that got pregnant in school, persevered and did not become another statistic because you decided that you wanted more in life and you went after it. As women and mothers you broke the barrier and should to tell others that they can do it too. It's important to have passion because it motivates you not to stay in conditions that are not your purpose or your destiny.

The Bible tells a story of Sarah and Abraham in the Voice translation of Genesis 21:9-11, it states; "But a damper was put on the day when Sarah saw the son Hagar (the Egyptian girl) bore for Abraham laughing and teasing her son. She became jealous and demanded of Abraham: Sarah: Throw this slave woman and her son out right now! The son of this slave is not going to share the inheritance along with my son, Isaac, if I have anything to do with it! Sarah's demand was extremely distressing to Abraham, since Ishmael was also his son." This sounds like "Baby Mama Drama and Abraham is caught in the middle." Sarah was the mother to one son, Hagar was the mother to the other son and Isaac was the father to both. This fight that began many years ago still exist today in that Ishmael is the father of the Arabic nation and Isaac is the father Hebraic/Israelite nation and according to the Word of God they will fight until Christ returns still over land and the rights they both should have had. These three consenting adults should have had a conversation about what this relationship would like. But God, being God, declared that He would bless both children.

"Sarah's demand was extremely distressing to Abraham, since Ishmael was also his son." This starts the Baby Daddy Drama. Genesis 21:14 – 17, the Voice translation says, "So Abraham got up early in the morning, took bread and a container of water, and gave them to Hagar. He placed them on her should, gave her the child – *his firstborn* – and sent her away. She left and wandered in the wilderness near Beersheba." Now, take a moment and think about this. Abraham, at this time was filthy rich and all he gave his firstborn child was bread and water. Do you see why the fighting started and continues to this day? Ishmael, who was thrown in the midst of consenting "adults", was trying to understand how could you do this when I am your son. Abraham sent no money, no servants, and no food and told them, in so many words; I don't know where you are going to go, but you have to get up out of here. Verses 15 - 16 read, "When the water in the container was all gone, in desperation she left the child under the shade of one of the bushes, Then she walked off and sat down opposite him, about a bowshot away. Hagar: I can't bear to watch my child die. Though Ishmael is about 16 years old at this time, she still considers him her child. As she sat there, she cried loudly." This is Hagar's demonstrative condition to indicate that she was suffering from PTSD. People are suffering and the church wants them to come in and shout over it, put more oil on their heads and cry. More has to be done and it starts with the pastors and down. We have oversimplified the conditions of PTSD. PTSD can cause people to snap or lose their mind and may lead to a desire to hurt or kill someone. True, the church cannot assess every situation and declare that it is the devil, but people are having real situations, real problems and we cannot keep acting as if the solution is resolved because they spent three minutes on the altar. People are in real trouble and dying and all the church is expected to do is to cut a shout and speak in tongues. There is no one that can get healed from that. We need to talk about these real problems and deal with them. Being real is being saved and dealing with these issues, just because we declare salvation does not mean we are not suffering in our homes from these conditions. Everyone has issues, but it's when these issues explode onto our news that we see a mother that has been convinced in her mind that it would be better to kill her children then to keep living the life that she is living. Living saved will change the outcome of life, but your life is still in process, daily. Hagar was about to leave her child under a shade tree because she could no longer handle the PTSD. What do you do when people try to tell you their issues? You can't just say that "I'll pray for you", no, that's not enough, we need real talk that's touching on real issues.

We as parents must work to create, mold and shape our children into what we believe they would be from the beginning. A five year old doesn't know what he will be when he is older he's just saying what he knows. In a kingdom, the parents begin grooming their child from the time that they are born to be king. There was no question as to what they would be, but many question later in life what your children have become. As a parent you never realize that where they are is where you left them. Perhaps you left them with a molesting babysitter or you walked away and left them alone. They have become defenseless and they are fighting just to be heard or for someone to know who they are, but it's because when they were a kid you did not teach them to be adults, but you taught them to be kids and to stay in their place.

P.M.S. (POWER, MONEY & SEX)

While you have been beating up on your kids saying ridiculous things like shut up, you're too stupid, you don't know what you're talking about, all these phrases are shaping who you're child will be.

In verse 16, out of desperation, Hagar cried out but God couldn't honor her prayer because her desperation had caused her to abandon her child and walk away. In desperation you can cry out to God, but God does not hear those who walk away from their assignment. But, "God heard the voice of young Ishmael, and a messenger of God called out to Hagar from heaven." God heard the child and He provided.

Clearly you can see that baby mama drama and baby daddy drama existed even in the Bible. If you're entering into a relationship, where children are involved, the children have to be top priority and the focus of any future decisions. The welfare of the child or children must come first. The two consenting adults cannot allow how they feel emotionally about one another to selfishly disturb or destroy the well-being of the child or children. If a man already has children by another woman and is now in a new relationship, with a new woman, and this new woman in this man's life cannot accept this man's child or children as a package deal, just like her child or children come as a package deal to the new man in her life, then this should be a red flag to the relationship.

This new woman in the man's life cannot expect this man to neglect the responsibility of taking care of his biological children, if she does then that's a red flag that this relationship is in trouble before it begins. There may be other red flags to look for but you should also consider this list of things to do or not do:

The first thing to do in a new relationship to avoid baby mama drama or baby daddy drama is to establish a networking system that works for everybody on both sides concerning the visitation rights for the child or children without having to get the courts involved.

The second thing to do if the mother or the father from the previous relationship is bitter or still emotionally hurt and damaged with resentment and retaliation and refuses to network or collaborate for the best interest of the child or children will be to get the courts and the law involved. At this point and only then would it be better to avoid the woman, the man or the children in the new relationship to keep them from getting hurt.

The third thing to watch or pay attention to as a woman getting into a new relationship is if you are about to date or marry a man with kids and his own kids don't want to be around him and he doesn't want to be around his own kids. It's because he's a dead beat dad and he doesn't take care of his own. How much more do you think that he will take care of your kids? These are warning signs to put you on alert. These signs could indicate how he will take care of your kids.

The fourth thing to watch and pay attention to as a man and you're about to marry a woman that has kids is if you are in the early stages of your relationship and she neglects her child or children like an unfit mother. Does she still like partying and hanging out more than nurturing her children and spending time with them? Buyers beware, because if this woman that you want to marry is neglecting her own children, how much more do you think that this woman, who neglected her own child or children will neglect you and not value you as a man in the relationship?

P.M.S. (POWER, MONEY & SEX)

The fifth thing to watch and pay attention to or to do as men is never allow the woman that you are now in the new relationship with, demand or convince you to not have a relationship with your other child or children from a previous relationship, but wants you to do for her child or children.

The sixth thing to watch and pay attention to as women is to stop using your child or children as a weapon to get back at that child or children's father because you have been hurt by the relationship.

The seventh thing to watch and pay attention to as men and what you should not do as women is to use your children as a bargaining chip to get a child support check to pay your bills and to buy your hair and clothes. These women do nothing for their child or children, of whom the money that they receive is for. The child support check is to be spent on the child, not the parent. It's called child support not your support!!!

The eighth thing not to do as a woman is to use your child or children to tear down their father because he left you to be with somebody else. This is called the boomerang effect.

The ninth thing not to do as a woman is to keep taking out hurt and anger on your children because you are angry and upset at the baby daddy. They are not a weapon to be used against their father.

The tenth thing to do as a woman and a mother is to remove your emotions and hurt feelings toward the baby daddy out of every decision that you make. Your decisions should be centered on benefiting the child or children, not around your hurt and emotions.

The eleventh and last thing women should not do is to bring everyone from the outside and the inside into the decisions that you are making for your child or children that will impact their future. Stop taking counsel or advice from someone that specializes in failure and take counsel from someone that specializes in success.

Reference: (2013, April California Broker). www.aflac.com., Life Lines; A Life-Changing Decision for Single Parents

Reference: (2007, Jan) www.ncbi.nlm.nih.gov —Mental health problems among single and partnered mothers. The role financial hardship and social support.

Baby Mama Drama Part 2

No More Drama, Drama Queens

Rachel and Leah are two sisters in love with the same man and the issues between these two sisters have caused them to become dysfunctional in life and to struggle to find their identity and purpose. Their relationship has become so toxic and led them to behave like "Drama Queens", women fighting to prove that they are better because of what they feel they can do better than the other. A Drama Queen is a person that loves being melodramatic always exaggerating and sensationalizing every minor thing in life. They over emotionalize and over think the minor things and make them major problems. A Drama Queen always advertises their business, the more public the better. They like to put everything they do on blast for the world to see. They like places such as face book, Snap Chat, Twitter, and other social media sites. The more people, that these "Drama Queens" can tell their issues too; the better.

Leah and Rachel became Drama Queens. They kept unnecessary drama going on 24/7. Leah is struggling from rejection and silent frustration which is an inward suppression that causes mood swings. Rachel is struggling for attention, she operates with an impulse disorder and suffers from being passive aggressive. These two sisters cannot co-exist together in life, because of a man. Their relationship with Jacob has led them to hating each other but like true "Drama Queens" still respecting good competition. They can still see the strengths of the other and it brings out the jealousy in both women. Leah is insecure and Rachel is a pre-madonna that is attractive and beautiful on the outside, but ugly on the inside. Rachel pretends to be more than she really is but she is unstable, insecure, and manipulative. She likes to portray that she is ghetto fabulous. Leah sees Rachel's beauty and love and how she has found favor with Jacob. Rachel sees that Leah is favored by God, fruitful and able to produce for Jacob when she can't. The interesting dynamic to this relationship is that Jacob himself is struggling in both of his relationships with these two women and within himself. He suffers from an identity crisis, attempting to be a "player" or "hustler", while all at the same time destroying the relationship between these two women.

Leah is so insecure that she cannot focus on raising her children as their mother because she continues chasing after a man that does not want her. She is stressed out and depressed over a man that rejects her and instead of making Jacob lover her, she causes him to lose respect for her and to possibly hate her. She thinks that if she traps him by having his babies he will love her more, but instead of making him love her more, he lost respect for her.

Jacob had been tricked and trapped into being in a relationship with Leah. He had been manipulated by his uncle, used by Leah to produce children for leverage and to be a pawn sacrificed, just to stay in her life. Leah's plan backfired; Jacob became angry and hateful toward her. Between Jacob's anger and hatred in his relationship, Leah's rejection issues and insecurities, their relationship was toxic, dysfunctional and unhealthy. The depth of these issues affected them and their children, especially the first four sons.

Leah had six sons by Jacob. The first four sons Leah had were to trap Jacob into loving and staying with here, a typical Drama Queen move, but Leah's actions caused her sons to suffer mental and emotional damage. Leah's mental and emotional disconnect from Jacob caused her to influence her children with her hurt and pain. She named her son Reuben which means to be unstable; miserable, or affliction caused by someone else's hurt or pain. The second son she named Simeon, which means unattractive, unloved and God heard me. Her third son, she named Levi meaning God has joined together what has been unattached and disconnected. It also means to join together by being different. Before Leah had her fourth son Judah she realized that being a Drama Queen would never get her what she wanted and who she needed most had already given her more then she could ask for. Leah realized while carrying Judah that she had to cut the cord and sever every ungodly soul tie. She stopped trying to please man and started praising God. Judah's name means praise and when she birthed Judah she broke the soul-tie within herself. Any relationship that mentally causes you to believe you need to trap a man is a toxic relationship.

There are five symptoms or indicators that you are in an unhealthy, toxic and dysfunctional relationship. If you are in a relationship that has a tendency to be domineering or dominated by your partner; whether he or she tries to think for you or to control all of your decision making abilities. If you are in a relationship that has a tendency to be passive aggressive and it begins to show signs of unusual mood swings, inconsistency or impulse disorders. A third symptom or sign is when your relationship demonstrates patterns of temper tantrums, out of control anger, and accusatory discussions or finger-pointing just to start an argument. When your relationship partner begins to use intimidation and fear tactics through mental, verbal and physical abuse, just to destroy your confidence, identity and purpose in life, by belittling you. The fifth symptom and maybe the one that could cost you or your partners life is the obsessive fatal attraction. When the one you love becomes the one you hate or when the person that you're with becomes an out of control lover and a jealous stalker. When an out of control lover turns into a stalker, that person has begun believing that what they are doing, (the stalking) is because of the love they have for you. They have become insecure and jealous and they begin keeping up with their partner to insure they don't get hurt. The out of control lover becomes abusive in the relationship and what they believe is love has become mentally deranged. They have become emotionally broken in their mind and this is how they are coping with what they see as just showing their partner that they love them and that they are there for them. The potential harm is signified by a lack of trust. This individual is so insecure that they have to always know where you are. They follow you to your job and they follow you to church, if they don't go with you. They follow you to your friend's home, your family's home and when they see you are not looking they go through your phone, your wallet or your purse looking for anything that would be a sign of cheating or distrust. If you are experiencing any of these symptoms, please reconsider your relationship and/or get out because this is not what God intended. As we explained in the first edition of P.M.S., God had a plan for man, a blueprint for his life, and as we have explained in this edition, God required man and woman to get an understanding prior to saying "I Do." In order to be a helpmeet you have to know (have an understanding) what your role is in the relationship and how you will carry out your part in this new relationship agreement in order for the partnership, relationship or business to work together and to achieve relationship success.

No longer can you be the "Drama Queen" fighting for some man's attention. You have a responsibility to yourself and to your children to get an understanding and to have an agreement. If that is not something your partner can come in alignment with then perhaps this is not the one because the "one" will come to the table with 100%, not half of anything. They will understand you, love you for you and they will love your children as their own. Your partner will be in agreement that they are priority and they will not be a by-product of your relationship. Jacob married Leah and then Rachel, he also slept with their concubines, Bilhah and Zilpah and from these relationships he had 13 children and because of the dysfunction of their parents and the toxicity of their relationship, all of these children suffered and grew up to have dysfunction in their own relationship.

Scripture References:

Genesis 29:30–35 AMP
Proverbs 22:24-25 EXB
Genesis 30:19-20 EXB
Genesis 30:21 EXB
Genesis 35:18–19 EXB
Genesis 30:9-11 EXB
Genesis 30:12-13 EXB
Genesis 30:7-8 EXB

P.M.S. (POWER, MONEY & SEX)

Author's Note:

This edition of the P.M.S. Factor was written to give you a greater understanding of relationships; personal, business, or community. This edition enhances the first P.M.S. Factor book by providing more clarity and more knowledge of the greatest thing needed for all relationships and that is an understanding promissory agreement. This book could have extended for many more chapters and at some point it may continue because of all that the Lord wants to say concerning relationships, but the goal was to touch on a major area that impacts many relationships and that many fail to consider first when entering into a relationship and that is gaining an understanding of who everyone in the relationship is and what role they will fulfill in the relationship. There truly is much more to add but we pray that you are blessed by the words of this book, and by the Spirit of God that has given utterance, and the anointing to say the things that were said and to teach the things that were taught. God's word has so much to offer concerning relationships, and we pray that this book will cause you to study and to learn more about what He has to say.

P.M.S. (POWER, MONEY & SEX)

We also would like to thank you for choosing this book to read. We know that you had many choices when you found this book, but we know that it was God's divine Spirit that led you to choose this book on relationships. So we thank you and pray that you will learn more about Senior Pastor Tommy Twitty online at www.trtministries.com, or at his local church website www.wodca.org.

About the Author:

Sr. Pastor Tommy R Twitty

"An anointed vessel of God,

seeking the heart of God for God's people"

A visionary, teacher, prophet, author, and founder of TRT Ministries, the TRT Network and Reaching Outside the Walls Ministry (ROTW). He is a native of Chesnee, South Carolina, and the Senior Pastor of Word of Deliverance Church in Gaffney, S.C. Apostle Twitty is a devoted husband to his lovely wife, Elect Lady Nicole Humphries Twitty, the father to their three beautiful children, Shante', Rashawn, and Amber and the grandfather to Braylon Twitty.

The Word of Deliverance Church is a youthful, multi-cultural, soul-winning ministry, with a message of love, healing and deliverance, where "All People of All Races are Freely Welcomed." Apostle Twitty's vision is to "work diligently to build the Saints, that the Saints build the City." The first step in the building process is to get people to understand that "if you change the way you think, you will change the way you live". With this vision in his heart, he is dedicated to "Reaching Outside The Walls" to seek out and save the lost, whatever the cost.

In 1998, God gave Pastor Twitty a vision to establish ROTW, to write and make plain the vision as He had instructed. God told Apostle Twitty to bring both the church and the world together to become the Kingdom of God. The mission of ROTW Ministries is to go out into the cities, cross over into other states, travel around the world, and to other nations, to restore, deliver, and liberate God's people, that they may declare unto themselves and others that they shall live and not die in the Kingdom of God.

God revealed to Pastor Twitty what the latter days would be like if he did what he believed was godly. He told him how to bring the world into the Kingdom of God. He told him how to lead the twentieth century church from its current state, how to dress her, arm her, and to equip her, that she may lose her traditional form and her religious status. Pastor Twitty was told to prepare for both a kingdom position and a priesthood role alongside men and women of God with the same vision. The vision is to bring the body of Christ together as one, that we may go outside the walls and begin the work of the kingdom, by gathering those who are lost in the system and have gotten entangled in the snares of the system. The "system" has failed us, but the Kingdom will enable the world and the church to come together.

As founder of TRT Ministries, Apostle Twitty has authored the book *Wait for It*, which is based upon Isaiah 40:31:

> *But they that wait upon the Lord shall renew their strength; they shall mount up with wings as eagles; they shall run, and not be weary; and they shall walk, and not faint.*

This book is based upon everyday living and is backed by God's Word. Apostle Twitty has taught several leadership series, but is most proud of the series "Making of a Leader" and *"The Nehemiah Strategic Planning Manual and Study Guide"*, in which he has taken the Word of God and the things of the spirit and made them applicable to the lives of everyday people who are seeking an understanding of God's plan for their lives. Apostle Twitty has also published the book *The Answer*, which is based upon the book of Nehemiah. This book provides you with answers to the questions for which you continue to seek God, as they relate to building your life, ministry, career, and business. Later, Apostle Twitty completed another book entitled, *The Revelation of Jesus, Characteristics of the Seven Churches*, a dynamic book for learning about the seven churches of Asia Minor and the time in which we are living.

God has blessed Apostle Twitty to be heard on the radio and to be seen on several television shows. He is becoming more and more involved in his role in the communities, as he builds upon the foundation of faith that God has given him. In spite of all that Apostle Twitty has accomplished, he always, without hesitation or reservation, gives God the glory, because he knows that nobody but God could have opened the doors that have been opened for him.